brave

this is me

Brave : This Is Me
Published by Orange, a division of The reThink Group, Inc.
5870 Charlotte Lane, Suite 300
Cumming, GA 30040 U.S.A.

The Orange logo is a registered trademark of The reThink Group, Inc.

Unless otherwise noted, scriptures taken from the Holy Bible, New International Version®, NIV®. Copyright © 1973, 1978, 1984, 2011 by Biblica, Inc.™ Used by permission of Zondervan. All rights reserved worldwide. www.zondervan.com The "NIV" and "New International Version" are trademarks registered in the United States Patent and Trademark Office by Biblica, Inc.™

Other Orange products are available online and direct from the publisher. Visit our website at www.WhatIsOrange.org for more resources like these.

ISBN: 978-1-63570-070-1

© 2018 Brave Global

Lead Writer: Lisa Knight

Project Manager: Nate Brandt

Printed in the United States of America

First Edition 2018
1 2 3 4 5 6 7 8 9 10
03/28/18

Introduction

>> WE ARE PUMPED THAT YOU HAVE TAKEN THIS JOURNAL. We are even more excited at the possibility of you reading and writing in it. Please mark it up. We've designed this journal as a way of starting a conversation. See, we believe that you have the ability and the potential to change the world. We really do. Maybe you're holding onto the lie that you can't make a difference. We've all had moments when we've questioned if we have what it takes. Sometimes it's because of the words of a parent or a classmate, or because of something we saw on social media. But we want you to know, no matter what hurtful things you've heard in the past, we're here to help you discover the truth.

The thing about the truth is that it always sets you free! But the journey of freedom begins on the inside. Truth is found deep within you. When you dig deep and are really hungry for real truth—you will find it and it will set you free. We know this because we've experienced it for ourselves.

This journal was not written by some person in an ivory tower trying to think about what you need to know. It was written by someone who has been where you are. Someone who has lived in 37 different foster homes. Someone who was told repeatedly by her own mother that she was not loved or wanted. Now, that person—who is LISA BARNES—is a BRAVE woman who has not only survived those circumstances, but is thriving! She spends her days helping other kids all around the world know that their story doesn't start or end with who their biological parents were—it starts and ends with what they were born for! Freedom baby.

So, when we sat down to start this process, we began with Lisa writing a letter to herself when she was 12. You may be interested in reading that on PAGE 5. When we started talking about this journal, Lisa starting wishing she had one when she was 12 years old. And that's when we knew that it was so important that you do.

So how does it work?

>> BRAVE. Bravery is not just one moment and one decision. It often starts out like that, but bravery is something that is developed in your everyday life. It's one big decision that has a thousand little decisions connected to it. Bravery is not just something that happens in your head – like a good decision you make. Bravery is made up of a series of BRAVE ACTS.

So, what we want you to do is think about some important things [thought section]– and then decide to act bravely [act section]. There will be some ACTS that accompany this journal.

Do them.

Write, draw, cry, laugh, color, share, try it out. We know for sure that BRAVE acts every day make you brave for life - that's how we got brave. We think it's time you knew it, too.

So, if it isn't clear yet, let us tell you one more time. You were born to change the world. You were born to overcome. You were born to help others. You were born because you are loved. You were born because you are wanted, needed, and invited. You were born to be BRAVE. Let the journey begin.

By Danielle Strickland
Social Justice Warrior

Letter From Lisa Herself

I was in 7th grade and things were a mess. My mom and I couldn't live together. She was hooked on drugs, and sick all the time. Most days it seemed like things wouldn't ever be better, like things couldn't ever change. On those days it felt like I had no one to turn to.

As I write this, I am a 32 year old adult. I'm married and have two kids of my own. I've made it out of that life that used to feel like it held me captive. A lot of older people say, "If I only knew then what I know now….." Then they talk about how things would be different.

For me, if I could go back and tell 12-year-old Lisa just one thing, it would be something simple...*You're not alone*.

If I could sit down and talk with her, here's what I would say, "Hey young Lisa, I know things are really rough right now. I know you wake up every morning afraid and unsure. I know that you go to school and do all you can to keep your home life a secret. I know that it seems like everyone else has it better than you do. I know that you feel lost and alone. *But you're not alone*.

There are lots of other kids who go to your school, kids that live in your neighborhood, and even kids that you don't know who are going through hard times. Sometimes it's hard to tell what other people are going through because it's human nature to want to hide the things about us we think are embarrassing, wrong, or difficult. Most people go through tough situations, and even though their lives may look different than yours, just know that when things are hard, others will understand. It's okay to share your hurts with people who are safe. You don't have to be tough all the time. You may even find a friend who can help you through - and you can help them too. We were created to journey through this together. *You're not alone*.

When things are hard at home, there are other people who can love you and be there for you. It may not be your family, but it could be teachers, or people at your church, maybe a friend's mom, an Aunt, or even foster parents. Look for people who are part of a much bigger family to step in and be what you need. You can have a family, even if it looks different than the families you see on TV, or the ones you see every day. *You're not alone*.

When it's dark at night and you feel afraid, or you are feeling like no one gets it, or even if you feel like no one is on your team, or you feel like you don't fit in, and no one cares...*You. Are. Never. Alone.*

That's because the creator of the universe, the dude who made everything—from every leaf that's ever existed, to the smallest ant, or even giant elephants—made you. He knows you and He loves you. He will always be with you and never ever leave you. And there is nothing you can do about that. *You're not alone*.

So young Lisa, you are loved. You are valuable. You are wanted. You will have a better life. But more than those things, even when you can't see it now, please know that in so many ways—*You're not alone*."

By Captain Lisa Barnes

[Chapter 1]
Who you are and why it matters

>> OUR LIVES ARE MUCH BIGGER THAN OURSELVES. From the beginning of time, there have been people who have had to fight to survive and to thrive. In the Bible, in Exodus 1, it talks about two chicks who had the job of being midwives - which meant that they were like the doctors that helped women have babies. This guy named Pharaoh, who was like the king of Egypt, was trying to do some shady population control by telling the midwives that they needed to kill all the boy babies, but let the girls live. The midwives didn't wanna do it, because they believed that God was legit, and He wouldn't be okay with hurting the innocent.

Then a bit later, the Pharaoh wanted to do the same kind of thing by throwing all the baby boys in the Nile River, and this is where we first meet baby Moses.

Brave thought

ORIGIN STORY: Moses first shows up on the scene. He's born at the time where the baby boys were all supposed to be killed by drowning. But his parents weren't down, so they hid him for as long as they could. When the circumstances changed and they just couldn't do anymore, that is when we see someone else stand up for him - his sister Miriam.

Exodus 2:4 "His sister stood at a distance to see what would happen to him".

What people do you have in your life that have stood at a distance? Who has made a difference or stood up for you when you needed it?

Brave Act

Write a fictional story about a person standing up for another person. Bonus points for describing how the one who needs standing up for may or may not be an oppressed person.

In verse 5, Pharaoh's daughter found Moses. It was her dad that was the bad guy in this story. In spite of living in the same house with the bad guy, she was brave and stood up for the baby and did what was right.

Brave Act

Make a list of reasons why it can sometimes be hard to do what is right. Make another list of good things that can happen from doing what is right.

Why can it be hard to do what's right?

What are good things that can happen from doing what's right?

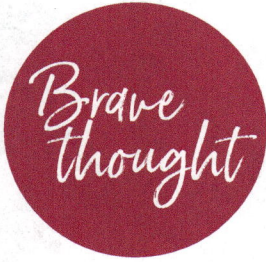

We've all come from somewhere. Your story isn't just about you. It's all the story of freedom and showing connectedness. The oppressor wants you to think that you are alone, and unloved, but the opposite is true. We are all in this together, and we all have stories and hurts. Hearing about our similarities and differences can unite us instead of dividing us.

What are some ways that we can connect to other people, to hear their origin stories and understand where we are all coming from?

Brave Act

We are one.

We are united.

We are together.

Brave thought

FAMILY DRAMA: Moses knew that he was different.
Verse 11 tells us that he saw his people being abused and he flipped out. He
was so mad, he even killed a guy. When Pharaoh found out that
Moses did this, Pharaoh tried to kill Moses, but Moses ran away.

No one's life is perfect. We all have hurts and pain in our stories.
Sometimes, like Moses, we may have even made big
mistakes that resulted in an unhappy ending.

We have all had stuff that's led us to the places we are now, both positive
and negative things. EVEN THE BAD THINGS CAN BE USED FOR GOOD.

Brave Act

Make a timeline of important things that have happened in your life in order as you can remember them. The positive things go on the top, and the negative things go on the bottom.

POSITIVE

As early as you can remember...to present day.

NEGATIVE

It can be hard to see the things that shaped us, especially the hard stuff all at once. BUT... there is good news. We can redeem the bad stuff.

Make a list of the negative things that have happened and then write any positives that have come from that.

BAD THING	GOOD THING
Example: My dog died.	I learned that even when sad things happen, it gets better and the hurt isn't forever.

Use this page to keep writing OR draw a picture of your favorite memory.

Remember that bravery is not the lack of fear, but the ability to move forward in spite of fear.

Brave thought

Life is big and full of things that affect us, even if we didn't choose them—even if they aren't our fault. But, life is full of a lot of small things too. Things that may seem insignificant, but when we take a closer look—we are able to see how important and special they really are. For example—our fingerprints. No one else in the history of this planet has the same fingerprint that you do. No one ever has and no one ever will. When you turn your hand over and see the different ridges and patterns on the tips of your fingers, those are reminders of how detailed the Creator of the universe was when He made you. He knows all about you from how many hairs you have on your head, to every curve and bend on your fingerprint. He knows us, and there isn't anything we can do to make Him know us or love us any less.

Get a washable marker and color on one of your finger tips, all the way from the first crease to the tip of your finger. While it's still wet, push it down firmly on the center of this page. Once you have your unique print there, think about some things that make you special or different from everyone else. And remember that those things were designed on purpose by something much bigger than ourselves. When you see those unique things, God sees them too, and He is proud of you.

Your Fingerprint Here:

What makes you special or different?

We are all individuals, and have our own set of gifts and abilities that really could change the world. That is still true even if life started out really rough—or even if we have parents that didn't love us or care for us like they should have.

There is a verse from the Bible; Isaiah 49:15 that says, "Can a mother forget the infant at her breast, walk away from the baby she bore? But even if mothers forget, I'd never forget you—never."

We know that God will never forget us because He made us. That's right, the Creator of the universe knows all about us - the good, the bad, and the ugly, and loves us just the same. God looks at us and He thinks, "This is exactly what I had in mind when I made her." God looks at you and is so proud of who you are becoming and can't wait to see the great things you are going to do to change the world.

No matter who forgets, or doesn't see you for who you are and the world altering potential you have, God sees. He knows. And He'll be by your side the whole way.

What do you think about that?

Brave Act

Make a list of times you feel like someone didn't follow up with their end of the deal or times where you feel forgotten. Then draw a line to one of the things that reminds us that God wouldn't ever do that to us.

Times when you felt like someone didn't follow through, or you felt sad or forgotten	Reminders that God wouldn't ever do those things to us:
	> We are loved.
	> We can be forgiven.
	> We can do great things.
	> The Bible says that even if our mothers forget, God won't ever.
	> We are smart.
	> We aren't alone.
	> We were created for a purpose.
	> God never changes.
	> We are funny.
	> Every person matters.
	> Our words have meaning and should be heard.
	> We can be restored.
	> We should all be safe.
	> We can be made new.
	> God knows all about us, even how many hairs we have on our head.
	> God is proud of us.
	> We have gifts and abilities that make us unique and valuable.
	> God looked at his creation and saw it was good.

Brave thought

What are things that cause you to lose track of time?

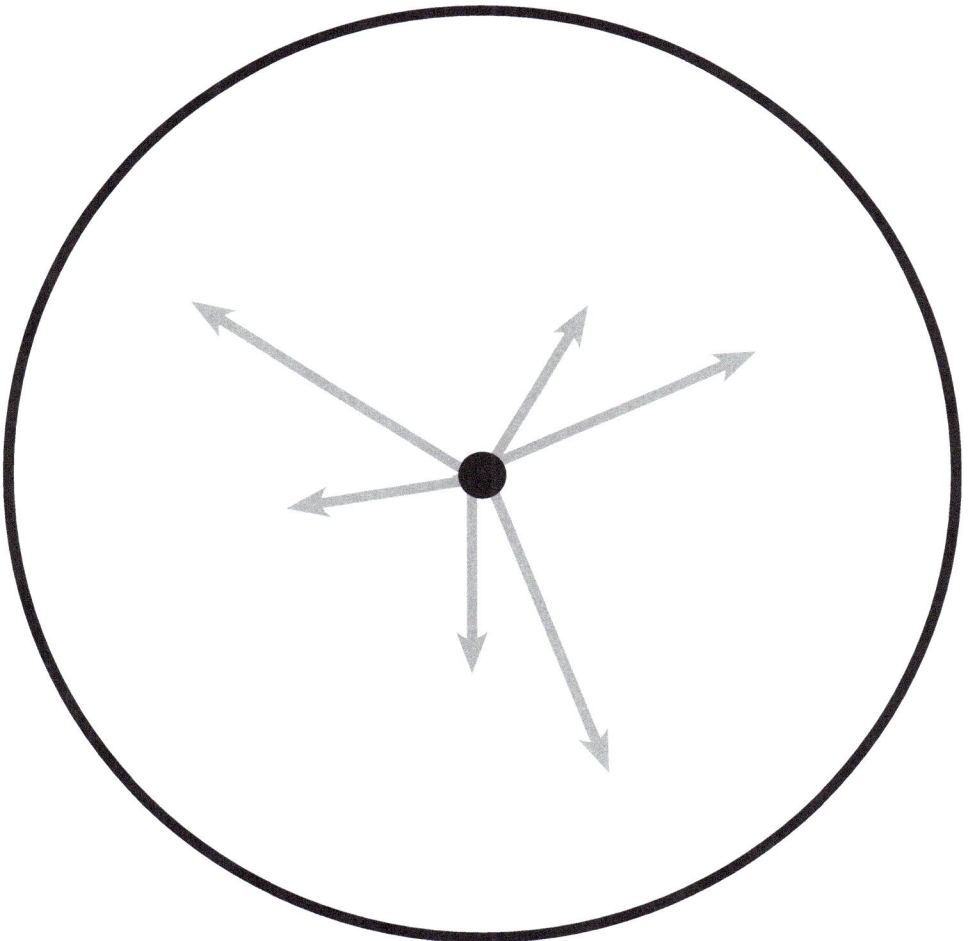

Brave thought

What are things that make you unique?

What are things that
make you laugh?

What are things you
like to study or learn
about?

[Chapter 2]
Who says so?
Battling the messages from others

Brave thought

What's in a name? Pharaoh's daughter named Moses his name because of what it means. It's about how he came to her. "I drew him out of the water."

Brave Act

What's your name? What does it mean? You may not know the story of why you got that name, but you can look it up and discover what the meaning is. Do this with your first and middle names. These meanings are a part of your identity. Learn them, celebrate them, live those meanings.

Example: Lisa = Devoted to God // Franziska = Free
Translation: Because I am devoted to God, I can be free.

Your first name: ....

Meaning: ....

Your middle name: ....

Meaning: ....

Translation: ....

THIS IS YOUR NAME. THIS IS PART OF YOUR IDENTITY. What else makes up your identity?

Who am I? Why am I?

"What lies behind us and what lies before us, are small matters compared to what lies within us."
— Emerson

In America, we are bombarded with images and opinions of who we are "supposed" to be, or what others think we should look like, or have interests in. The good news is that no one else needs to define us aside from the one who created us, and when He looks at us, He is so proud of who we are and who we are becoming.

Brave thought

Has anyone ever tried to change you, or make you into something you aren't?

Draw or describe what that was like in the boxes below:

Brave Act

Let's talk about some of the lies we are told by our world.

Make a table with 3 columns. 1st column—lies we are told, 2nd column—why they aren't true, 3rd column—a real truth we can put in place of that lie. These lies can be about our appearances, preferences, possible goals, or anything you can think of.

Example:

1st column—*You have to be a certain size to be considered beautiful.*

2nd column—*Beauty is very subjective and people can be beautiful for lots of different reasons.*

3rd column—*Someone is beautiful because of their kindness and character. Size doesn't matter at all.*

Lies we are told	Why they aren't true	A real truth that can replace the lie

We see pictures of celebrities online or in magazines that seem like they are fabulous and flawless. We may feel like that is what we are supposed to look like—and that we should do anything to get there. Maybe we think if they can do it so can we, and we have to.

A lot of the time the pictures we are using like a "how to be cute" reference guide aren't even real! They have been changed and edited to make people look like they have zero imperfections.

Do a little research on pictures before and after photo editing. See what people change, and how before the pictures were edited—they look very different, and spend time thinking about how you are great just the way you are.

Before Photoshop

After Photoshop

What are some things (both internal and external) that you like about yourself?

Brave thought

When there are so many mixed messages coming through about who we are and what we should be, we can sometimes tell ourselves lies as we try to figure out the truth about who we really are.

One of the lies some girls tell themselves is that there can only be one girl in charge. If we want to be in charge, we might belittle other girls in our circle, call each other names to put each other down, or crush the potential in others.

Sometimes we do this by bullying, name calling, or by spreading rumors.

Brave Act

Draw a picture of a way that some girls treat other girls poorly to be the main girl in charge. (Maybe this has been something you've done, or something that's been done to you.)"

How do you handle feeling tired, anxious, or stressed out? Many people do negative things to combat these feelings—sometimes people eat their feelings, hurt their bodies, or seek out physical attention from others to forget or minimize pain in their lives. What are some positive things you do as a reaction to these feelings? What are some negative things you do? What are some positive things that you would like to start doing as a response to these kinds of feelings?

Positive reactions
to negative feelings

Negative reactions
to negative feelings

Practice, Practice, Practice!

Practice the good. Out of the list of good responses to stress and negative feelings, take some time to practice them with yourself or with a friend. Strengthen these responses so they become your go-to actions during hard times. Write a bit about what these practices felt like and what some of your thoughts were.

Feelings? Thoughts?

Brave Act

Brave thought

Ch - Ch - Changes!

Our brains are amazing things. Let's get a little science-y for a minute. There is something that everyone with a brain has, and that is called neuroplasticity. This means when we develop habits, or one way of doing things—it makes a path in our brain. Example: If you walk the same way to school or work every day, it becomes a habit and you almost don't even have to think about it. Your brain can almost get there without much thought. If you decided to walk a new way, it would take lots of thought and it would feel very different. If you kept going that new way, it would create a new neuropathway in your brain. You can use this technique to change habits or thought patterns.

Let's do these steps together. First, think of a negative habit you'd like to change and why. Now, let's walk through this exercise together. I'll use nail biting as an example, but don't be afraid to think creatively about answers specific to you.

What's the habit you want to change?

What is the bad habit doing to your life, that would make you want to change it? **Example:** *Nail biting leaves us with sore fingernails, and instead of relieving nervousness and stress, it can often make us feel worse.*

Why change?

Take the attention away from the negative. **Example:** *Don't think, "Stop biting your nails! It's so gross!" as a way to change your behavior. Instead think, "You don't need to bite your nails anymore. Instead you can take some deep breaths to relax."* And before you know it you are going to be able to paint them all kinds of great colors. Daydream about what the first color will be.

Brave Act

New thoughts?

_____

_____

_____

_____

_____

_____

_____

_____

_____

_____

_____

_____

Who can help?

Ask for help from God and from friends. You don't have to do any of this alone. You have God in your corner, and that power can give you support to do all kinds of great things. <u>Example:</u> *Say, "God, help me break the habit of _____ . Help me to instead turn to You when I'm feeling anxious, nervous, or stressed. Thank you for helping me focus on you and other good things in my life."* You can also ask friends to call you out when they see you doing it.

Celebrate!!!

When you notice that you are behaving differently, and not doing the negative behavior as much, or maybe not at all—celebrate your accomplishments. <u>Example:</u> *When you think, "Oh, I haven't bitten my nails in 3 days!"* Give yourself a pat on the back, tell yourself good job, and know that you are doing things and moving in the right direction.

Who Runs the World? GIRLS!

To quote the famous modern philosopher, Beyoncé, "Who runs the world? GIRLS!" Girls make great leaders! But we have to watch out because sometimes when we're seen as leaders, it can be tempting to want to be the only one in charge. Some have the thought that there has to be one girl as the leader, and no one else is allowed. Which is a crazy thing! Instead of putting each other down, we should empower each other, and encourage each other to do great things. We don't have to compete. We can all do this and accomplish great things together.

What do you want to accomplish?

Make a plan to do something great. Make up a dance. Write a small play. Organize a clean-up event. Do something you are passionate about, and take along as many girls with you as you can. Empower your friends and girls you know to do great things, too. Watch for ways to help others succeed and don't forget that we all have the potential to make a difference.

Who is going to partner with you?

Brave Act

Do you need any supplies?

_____

_____

_____

_____

_____

_____

How will you get supplies
and information out?

_____

_____

_____

_____

_____

_____

How much time do you need to
accomplish this task?

_____

_____

_____

_____

_____

_____

What are you going to do
once you have succeeded?

_____

_____

_____

_____

_____

_____

Brave thought

Our bodies are not currency. Girls get a lot of cultural messages that tell us that we can use our bodies to get what we want, or to make guys like us. That couldn't be further from the truth. Our bodies are meant to be used to take us places we want to go, and be who we want to be. It's wrong to feel like we have to use our bodies to be important or loved. We are much more than that. Many friends I know were sexually abused (1 in 3 girls in America have this experience). Have you been sexually abused? That means that someone touched you in a sexual way that you didn't say yes to. This hurts physically and emotionally. The best way to deal with this is to get help. Who can you tell? Where can you go for help?

HELPLINE: 1-800-565-HOPE (4673)
More help for kids: 1-866-FORLIGHT (367-5444)

Make a list of all the things that our bodies do that bring you joy and make you feel strong or smart. Things like going on a run, climbing, drawing, etc.

Brave Act

Draw a picture of you doing the thing
that makes you feel the most
EMPOWERED & POWERFUL.

It's good to do uncomfortable things. It's weight training for life.

— Anne Lamott

The Power of Words

Brave thought

>> SELF-TALK MATTERS. **Our words have power, even the ones that we keep on the inside.**

Your **beliefs** become your **thoughts.**
Your **thoughts** become your **words.**
Your **words** become your **actions.**
Your **actions** become your **habits.**
Your **habits** become your **values.**
Your **values** become your **destiny.**
—**Mahatma Gandhi**

Famous words about words

What other quotes about our words have you heard?

In these thought bubbles, write thoughts you think regularly.

The good. The bad. And, the ugly.

My thoughts

Brave thought

How would life be different if you thought positive thoughts more frequently?

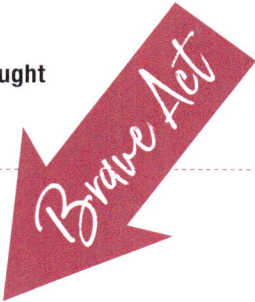

Brave Act

Draw yourself having a bad day

Write good thoughts you could think instead of the regular bad ones

Sticks and stones can break my bones and words can hurt the soul too.
Sometimes we don't realize the pain that we can inflict with our hurtful words, and sometimes we do know how much our words can hurt, and we do it on purpose. To be mindful of how our words have the power to hurt, do this exercise.

Put a rubber band on your wrist. Every time you say something rude, hurtful, disrespectful, or anything else you'd rather not have as part of your vocabulary, snap the rubber band, not enough to cause damage, but enough to sting and remind you that its better to not say those things. This can also be a helpful excercise for resisting the urge to harm yourself physically.

Brave Act

SNAP

Do this for a full day, and write some of the things you said that caused you to snap the band. You can color this in any way you like.

No complaining allowed. Are you ready for a challenge? For the next 30, days no complaining allowed. Those kinds of words can do damage too, but complaints damage ourselves more than others.

Brave thought

Brave Act

Can you remember all the things you complained about today? Write a list of all the negative things that came out of your mouth. What do you think when you see them all on paper?

Lemon Pledge

Every day is chance to live differently and sometimes complaining sets us back.

Are you up for a challenge? Let's start with doing our best for one day to limit complaining and negative talk.

After you do one day, try for two, then maybe three. You've got this!

Everyone talks to themselves. Some do it with their mouths out loud, but most of us just do it in our minds. We have what is called an internal dialogue going on all day. If we aren't careful, that internal dialogue could run us, but we remember that we are in charge of the dialogue. Picture you in your mind holding the wheel of your thought car. You are in charge when you hold the wheel. If you let go, the thought car will go crazy. So as you go about your day, regularly check that you are holding on to the wheel, and you are in charge of your thoughts.

Draw a picture of you in your thought car.

I like to turn my thoughts into prayers. It looks like this:

Old Way

"Oh man, it's time to wake up already? I don't want to go to school today. I have math, and I suck at that. I wonder if my friends are going to be there, or out sick still…"

New Way

"Hey God. Thanks for waking me up today. Thanks in advance for today. I'm a little tired still, so please give me the energy to keep going. I don't really love school. It's hard and there is a lot I don't feel like I understand. Help me to open my mind and to do my best. Help my teachers to help me when I need it. Be with my friends too. They have been sick, and I want them to be back to normal again."

Brave Act

Try this kind of thinking shift, and after a day of trying, write what you would have thought in the old way, when maybe you weren't holding on to the thought wheel, and then write the new way—with you in charge. Did you feel anything different? Is this something you might want to keep doing?

INTENTIONAL KINDNESS: Spend the day saying nice things. Say kind things with the purpose of making someone's day. Everybody is a somebody. Everybody needs to be treated with kindness, and you might be the only person sharing a kind word with them today.

What are some nice things people have said to you?

Here's a list of compliments and nice things you could say today. Circle the one you are going to try to use. Once you've done it, write about what it was like, and how people responded to it.

Compliments that aren't about physical appearance.

1. You're empowering.
2. I like your voice.
3. You're strong.
4. I think your ideas/beliefs matter.
5. I'm so happy you exist.
6. More people should be listening to what you have to say.
7. You're a very warm-hearted person.
8. It's nice seeing such kindness.
9. You're very down to earth.
10. You have a beautiful soul.
11. You inspire me to become a better person.
12. Our conversations bring me a lot of joy.
13. It's good to see someone care so much.
14. You're so understanding.
15. You matter a lot to me.
16. You're important even if you don't think so.
17. You're intelligent.
18. Your passion is contagious.
19. Your confidence is refreshing.
20. You restore my faith in humanity.
21. You're great at being creative.
22. You're so talented at _____.
24. You have great taste in _____.

[Chapter 3]
You Get What You Aim For

Brave thought

>> IF OUR DREAMS DON'T SCARE US, WE AREN'T DREAMING BIG ENOUGH. **The Creator of the universe wants us to accomplish great things. He has given us His son and His strength to change the world for good, and there isn't anything that could stop us… except ourselves—our doubt and our fear. If you could do anything to change the world for good, what would it be? No limitations. No obstacles. No fear.**

Brave Act

Brainstorm a list of things you would want to do to make the world a better place. Some can be for the future, but make some that you could do right now. Circle your top 3.

Brave Act

Do some research on young people who have done great things. They could be people who have done charitable work, created art, helped feed the hungry, or spoken up for those who don't have a voice.

Draw a picture of one of them accomplishing their dream.

Brave thought

What are things you've done that you are really proud of? It doesn't have to be something huge to be recognized as great. It could be doing well in school, or having a conversation with someone where you kept your cool when you felt like flipping out.

In each shape, write something you have done that you're proud of. Every day find a way to acknowledge the good of who you are, and what you can do.

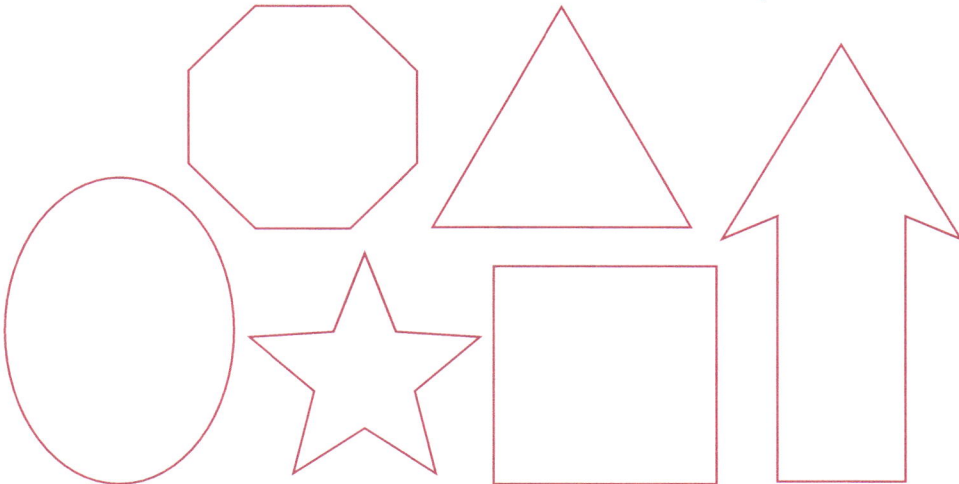

Brave Act

Brave thought

What would happen if you pushed yourself a little harder? Not saying that what you've done isn't good enough, but asking—how would things be different in your life if you gave 5% more in what you do?

Examples: Think a little harder before guessing on a test. Be just a little kinder when someone is getting on your nerves. Do your homework, and maybe a little extra credit.

Brave Act

Pick 3 things you can do today to push yourself a little harder. Write about what you did, what you felt, and if you see any positive change from giving a little extra.

Brave thought

We are strong women. Whether you are quiet or outgoing, whether you are easily embarrassed or love being the center of attention, or whether you love sports, art, or both, it doesn't matter. No matter who you are or what your personality is, there isn't anything you can't do. You are strong and smart and capable.

Write a fictional story of a character based off of yourself who accomplishes something amazing.

Brave Act

Brave Act

How does this make you feel? When you think about how you are powerful and strong, what kinds of things go through your mind?

Brave thought

You can have any job or career that you want. If you could be anything in the world, what would that be?

Draw a picture of you, proud and strong, doing your dream job. Do you wear a specific uniform like a police officer? Do you need specific tools like an artist or architect? Draw all of that here.

Brave Act

Now that you are thinking about what type of career you want to have (just know that you can change your mind at any time, and a lot of adults even change their minds. So no pressure to stick to this forever), what do you need to get there? Do you need to take specialized classes, join a club, or find someone to mentor you?

What will it take for you to accomplish your dreams? Do some research on what that job needs. Is it college? What different universities offer programs in that field of study? Do an internet search on which colleges you might attend to accomplish your dreams. Day dream about going there. Picture yourself walking to your classes and laughing with your new friends. Write a list of things you are looking forward to when you dream about this future.

Brave Act

School costs money, but there are lots of opportunities for that to happen. Money shouldn't ever get in the way of accomplishing your dreams. Don't give up because it can be expensive.

Brave thought

Brave Act

Do some research on scholarships and grants. If this applies to you, look for opportunities for kids who have spent time in the foster care system or who need financial aid. Some states give free scholarships for state universities for these kids. Look into this, and use this as a spring board to dream your big, sometimes scary, but still achievable dreams.

What websites did you visit?

What info did you learn?

Are there people you can talk to that will help social workers or school counselors?

There are times when we all feel like we can't do something. Maybe we feel too tired, sad, not smart enough, or too alone. If you have been here, you aren't alone in those feelings.

Write about a time where you felt like you couldn't keep going. What are things that make you feel like you can only go so far? What are things that make you feel like you have to quit?

Brave Act

Brave Act

What are things you could think or do when those feelings come up? What can you do to keep pressing forward even when it's hard, or you feel like you have every reason to give up?

Write words of affirmation on the lines below. Affirmations are positive things you may need to hear when you are feeling at your worst. To get started, think about what words or phrases would help you feel brave and strong on the days you feel tired and sad. What would keep you going?

Brave Act

Brave thought

Haters are gonna hate. No matter who we are or what we've done, there are always going to be haters in our lives. There will be people who say unkind words, think we can't accomplish great things, or question if we are crazy for aiming high. Instead of getting discouraged by them, let's be prepared for them.

When people criticize you for doing well or make fun of you for trying hard, what are you going to say to them? What are you going to say in your internal dialogue so they don't get to you?

Brave Act

Things to say to the haters that will stand up for yourself, while not adding to the drama.

Things you can think that keeps their negativity out and your confidence and positivity in.

There is a girl named Malala Yousafzai. When the taliban banned girls from attending school, Malala went anyway. She was shot for doing this, but survived. Malala is an advocate for girls everywhere and even won a Nobel Peace Prize.

Draw a picture of yourself
standing up for the oppressed.

Brave Act

"One child,
one teacher, one book,
one pen can change
the world."

— Malala Yousafzai

Chapter 5

Self Care and Why it Matters

Brave thought

>> WE HAVE FEELINGS AND THEY ALL MATTER.

Everyone has a story. In many of those stories, there's hurt, shame, or guilt that comes from what has happened in the past. But there is good news!
Those negative feelings do not have to define us. No matter what has been, we are new creations. Every day is a fresh start.

On the next page, color a picture of a butterfly. Before it was a butterfly, it was a caterpillar, which is really a dressed up worm. Then it lived in a hard shell, its cocoon. While it was in the cocoon, it changed into something totally different. It became beautiful—but it also grew wings. Able to now fly, it could help pollenate flowers and plants. The butterfly wasn't just beautiful. It was created with a purpose, and it does things that no other insect or animal can do. While you color it, spend time thinking about your purpose, and the hard things you have gone through to get where you are.
You aren't who you were. Today is your fresh start.

Brave Act

You aren't who you were.

Today is your fresh start.

Brave thought

We can't ignore the things that have hurt us. We have to face the past. Bad things may have happened to you, and it's okay to admit they are real. We can't heal and be whole if we act like they never happened. This process sucks. It is hard, and not for whimps. Start small today by picking just one thing that has happened to you that was painful. Look at it and address it as a brave and strong woman. Even if it hurts (because it probably will), know you can do this.

Brave Act

On the next page, write out the one thing you chose. Write the whole thing. Write what happened, how you felt, what you did or said or didn't do. Write it all out, and once it is written, color over the whole page with a dark marker or crayon. Then make something beautiful with it on the next page.

Even our hurts and
wounds can be made into
something beautiful.

Take the last page, full of your hurt and rip it up into small pieces,
about the size of dimes. Then using a glue stick or tape, fill them in this heart.
As you do that think, about how our hearts can be full and whole, even if they
have been hurt. You are bigger than the hurt. You can be whole again.

There may have been times in your life where you might feel like you've been treated like trash. You have great worth and value, and no matter how you've been treated—you aren't trash. You are something great, created by someone great.

Draw a picture of something beautiful coming out of something not so beautiful. Examples: a flower growing from a crack in the pavement. A butterfly landing on a skull. When you draw, spend time thinking about how we can be different than our surroundings or where we have come from.

If we don't take the time to really face our pasts, our hurts, and our mistakes—there is a good chance that those types of things will keep happening in our lives.

Brave Act

I WISH IT WERE DIFFERENT. Think of something in your past that bothers you. This could be something that was done to you, or something that you did, and causes you regret. Now imagine that story happens, but this time it has a different ending. Write out the story, and give it a new ending. What had to change to make the ending different? How could you keep this new change in your mind the next time something like this happens?

We can look at our wounds and our hurts on our own, but there may come a time where we need help to heal completely. This often comes in the form of counseling. There is no shame in needing help. The strongest people get help from those around them.

Brave Act

Do some research about resources in your area that help and support people just like you. Try to find counselors, support groups, clubs, or anything that your city or town might have to help you keep on the journey to total healing. Make a list of those resources below.

Brave thought

This is hard work. Sometimes when things get too tough, you have to stop, take a break, and come back when you feel refreshed.

Brave Act

Make a list of things that relax and refresh you, and why that thing is helpful. Then take time to do one of those things before you go any further.

If we have hurts and wounds from our past and we don't deal with them, they don't just go away. It is almost like as we grow and mature, we build a house. It may be a really nice house, but if we don't deal with the junk, it's as if we've built our house on a sewer. The stink of what was will linger, no matter how hard we try to ignore it.

Draw a picture of your dream house. While you draw, think of things that you would need to heal from, things that keep hurting your feelings for impacting your life negatively. What do you think you need to do to free yourselves from them?

Brave Act

Brave thought

YOU ARE PRICELESS.
No matter who you are, what you look like, or what your life has been like, you are priceless. You have more worth or value than words can describe. You can't do anything to increase or decrease your value. Even if you do great and amazing things, or make huge mistakes—you will always be valuable and priceless.

Brave Act

Write all over this page words of affirmation. Things that describe your worth and value.
Examples: I am smart. I am lovable. I am worth it, etc.

Being BRAVE
does not mean you
live life without fear.
Being Brave means
you just move anyway.

~ Lisa Barnes

[Chapter 6]

The Hole in Your Heart, and How to Fill It

Brave thought

>> SOME OF US HAVE HAD THINGS HAPPEN TO US THAT SHOULDN'T EVER HAPPEN TO ANYONE EVER. Some of us have been physically hurt, emotionally wounded, abandoned, abused, and a lot of other things that leave us feeling like we are beyond repair. But, we can redeem the memory of those hurtful things—from the biggest hurt to the smallest insult.

Picture a memory where you got hurt somehow. Now picture an older, more mature version of yourself sitting next to the younger, hurting, more vulnerable you. Imagine you have a chance to tell the hurting you all the things you would need to hear right then to be okay. Maybe things like, "I know that you are sad right now, but things are going to get better." Or, "This hurt isn't going to last forever, there will be brighter days." Or, "This isn't your fault." Or, "You don't deserve this."

Brave Act

Imagine saying whatever it is that would change the memory of that hurtful time. Now when you think back to that memory, you aren't there alone. There is someone there to help you—and that someone is you. You are strong. You can get through this—even if your main resource is yourself. On the next page, write about what this exercise felt like. Do you think this kind of thing is helpful? Are there more memories that you may want to do this with?

Lets say I have a $100 bill. It's crisp and new. The corners are still perfectly straight, and it doesn't even smell dirty yet. If I offered it to you, expecting nothing in return, would you take it? *I would.* What if I took that perfect $100 bill and folded it into a little box, or an origami crane. Would you want it then? *I would.* What if I crumbled it up in a little ball? Would you want it then? *I would.* What if I spit on it? What about then? *I would still want it.* That crumbled up $100 bill was still the same one that we started with. It still has the same value. No matter how crumbled up you feel, your worth and value doesn't change. Not now, not ever.

Draw a picture of a made up bill. It could be for any amount. Draw your face, or something that symbolizes you in the center, then keep drawing things that are special to you, or that you think help describe your worth and value. No matter what happens to you, your value can not be taken away.

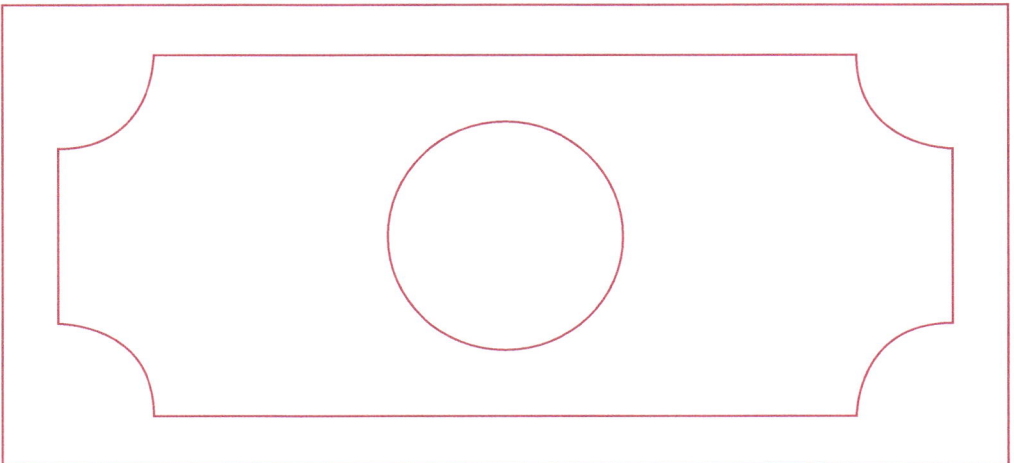

Poems are a great way to express ourselves. Take these next two pages and write down some poems that make you feel strong. They can be someone else's work or your own. They can be verses from the Bible, things you've heard before, or short encouragements you've seen on social media.

Day dream about an adult you. This version of the adult you is really great.
She is smart and confident, has great friends, and is really happy.

Draw a picture of the adult you on this page. On the next page, write a story about
what it took for you to get to this place, as the happy/healed/healthy adult you.

Brave Act

What it took to get to this place...

Let's say you have a friend who's just been hurt. Because you love her and want her to be okay, you go to her and tell her what she needs to hear right now. As we work toward being okay and getting stronger, we can help others who face things similar to what we have experienced.

Write a story of you comforting a friend. What do you say to her, how do you say it to her, and what happens after? This can be something that has really happened, or something that you want to make sure you are ready to do whenever you have the chance.

Brave Act

Sometimes we try to do things to make ourselves feel better, that really just make us feel worse. Things like sex, or too much physical contact. Sometimes we eat our feelings, and end up feeling yuckier than we did before. Sometimes we exercise until our bodies feel like they can't take one more step. Sometimes people even cut, or do some other kind of self- harm to their bodies. Can you relate to any of these things?

Brave thought

Brave Act

Think about a possible time where in an attempt to help yourself, you really hurt yourself instead. Describe that. What did you feel like after? Next time the thought to do that comes to mind, what is something you could do instead? How can you put steps into action that will REALLY help, instead of hurting more?

You aren't alone in this. Everyone has wounds and hurts and scars. Please don't feel like your story makes you different in a bad way. Everyone around you has hurt, but everyone's journey is different.

If you have a friend that you trust, take the time to get to know some of their story— maybe some of their hurt. Why do they do what they do, and feel what they feel? Help them to know you that way too, and see what you can do together to keep getting better and better.

Brave Act

Brave
thought

You are moving forward! Celebrate how far you've come already.

Describe growth in your life. What are some
ways that you are improving? Even if they are small
ways, or small changes—take time to celebrate it all!
Write about how far you've come.

Brave Act

I am not what
happened to me,
I am what I chose
to become.

— Carl Jung

Chapter 7

Defying Normal

>> THERE HAVE BEEN STUDIES DONE ABOUT PEOPLE WHO HAVE HAD CRAZY CHILDHOODS, **but have grown up to accomplish great things—and live very different lives. Out of all of the ways to describe these people, they all have at least these 3 things in common.**

[1] The knowledge that they are different. Sometimes that means that they feel like they don't fit in with their families, or others around them. They know that they are set apart for something.

[2] They feel very hopeful that life can be different. They don't feel trapped by their hurts, or like life has to look like that forever.

[3] They find ways to connect to people that they aren't related to. They know that relationships with friends, and people who are like family are really important, and that people don't have to share the same last name in order to come together.

Lets look at each of those, and see what you think, or how it may fit into your life (write your thoughts on the next page).

Brave Act

I'm different...

Life can be different...

Who to connect with...

Brave thought

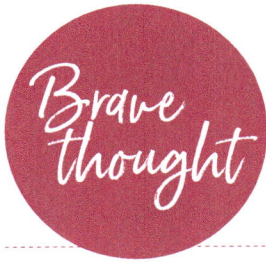

Being healed and whole doesn't mean that you look like everyone else, or you want the same things as everyone else. You were made to be unique, and there are things you can do that no one else on the planet can.

Make a list of the things that make you different, and why you love them. They could be external characteristics, or things that are a part of your personality. You choose!

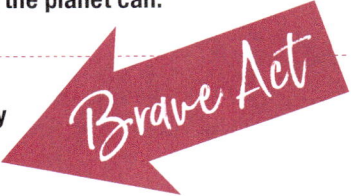

Brave Act

Has there been a time where you felt like maybe you were secretly adopted, or even an alien? Have you ever felt like you just don't fit in or belong somewhere?

Draw some scenes of what that looked like, and how it felt.

Brave Act

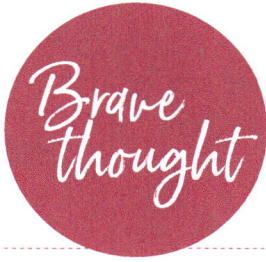

Why is fitting in important? It seems like people work really hard to blend in with everyone else. Why is this a priority for so many people? Is it a priority for you? Why or why not?

Answer the above questions, and journal about why we want to or not want to fit in, and who we want to fit in with.

Brave Act

Generally speaking, why is fitting in important?

When is it good not to fit in?

The glass is half full! Being positive, even in really junky situations can change a lot of things. Even if the biggest change is in ourselves.

Write in the water things that you can be positive about. What is going on that is really good, or maybe things that you can choose to look at in a positive light?

Brave Act

Write a list of situations where external situations stay the same, but it would be different if you were different. What are situations where you could increase your positive attitude and lighten the load a little bit?

Brave Act

Every day is a new day. Every day is a fresh start. Every day is a chance to live better or differently than we did the day before. If you could change anything from yesterday (things that are in your power to change - not what someone else did, or the weather or things like that) what would it be?

Make a list of things you did, or thoughts you had, or ways you responded to others yesterday that you would change if you could live tomorrow over again. Once you have the list of things you want to do over, scratch them out and write what you could have done differently, then plan to do that next time you're in this situation.

Brave Act

Things I've done	Things I'd do differently

There is a quote that says, "You can be mad in your pants, or you can be glad in your pants; but either way, you have to be in your pants." Sometimes the only thing we can change in a situation is our attitude; that even stands when the situation is really stinky.

Brave thought

Brave Act

Think about situations you have been in, are in now, or might be in the future that aren't that great. Write a few stories (past, present, and future) and a make believe response for how you can be glad, even if your situation sucks.

Brave thought

SPREAD THAT POSITIVITY AROUND.

Being a kind and positive person is contagious. Once people spend enough time around you, having a positive outlook will be something they want to have too. One way to intentionally spread this around is to reverse pickpocket, an idea that came from Rainn Wilson. (Plays Dwight in "The Office" and Founder of soulpancake.com)

You may have heard of pickpocketing before. This is never a good idea. Pickpocketing is when you reach into someones pockets or bag, and steal something. THIS IS NOT WHAT WE ARE ASKING YOU TO DO! Instead of taking something, you are going to leave something. We suggest writing a kind note. It doesn't have to be long or drawn out. It can be short and sweet, one sentence even. Something that someone can read and know that they are cared for by someone.

Leave it in a friend's desk, or stick in a school locker. Maybe even leave it in the fridge for a family member to find.

Brave Act

Use the next two pages to write and cut out your kind note.

You aren't alone. We all need people to journey through this life with us. Sometimes that can be our blood family, but it doesn't have to be. Who do you have in your life that you think you could connect with in a deeper way? A teacher, someone from church, or a group you are a part of? Who can you reach out to that you already know to take your life to a more intentional level?

Brave Act

Spend time thinking about who you already have in your lives that would make sense and not be strange to ask them to mentor you, or journey closer by your side.

Write out what you would like to say to them, and what you would want from them. Remember that people aren't mind readers, and it would be important for you to tell them what you need or want. Then do it. Present them with this idea and see what they think.

Write down on the next two pages how it went. Remember, this may not go just the way you want it to on the first shot. Even if it doesn't, don't give up. Find someone else to fill in this gap.

What you'd like to say...

How it went...

Earlier in this journal we talked about a guy named Moses from the Bible. Moses is a lot like a foster kid. He lived with his family for a little while, but then he had to live with another family. His life was never easy, but it was a little better because he had someone looking out for him. This person was Miriam, his older sister. When Moses' mom put him in the basket and sent it down the river, Miriam followed close by to make sure Moses was okay. When the basket drifted to Pharoah's daughter, it was Miriam who said she could help because she knew a mother who could nurse the baby until he was older (they didn't have formula back then, so it was common to have people nurse a baby when the birth mom wasn't around, or couldn't).

Miriam stuck by Moses. She journeyed with him, spoke on his behalf, and helped him along the way.

In our lives, it is important for us to have our own "Miriams." People who love us and want the best for us. This doesn't always mean that we agree all the time, or that we are best friends, but these people are like parents without being blood parents.

Brave Act

Do you have any Miriams in your life? Who has tried to speak truth into your situation, even if maybe you thought they were wrong, or didn't like their approach? This might have been someone else in the family, or a distant relative. Maybe it's a grandmother, foster parent, social worker, or teacher. On the next page, describe what that has been like—what you thought about it then, what you think about it now, and if you think it is important to have people like this in your life now.

Brave thought

You may not have had any of these kinds of people in your life yet. But don't worry! It isn't too late, and a lot of people walk alone until they are a little older. If you haven't found them yet, or you'd like to add another to your circle, let's take some time to brainstorm how to get these kinds of people in your life today.

Brainstorm categories

Why would I want someone to mentor me?
What would I want them to do or say?
What part would they have in my life?
Where would we go or what would we do?
How long would they be in my life?
Where are some places I could go to find them?
How would I get the conversation started?
Who are some people I think may fit for this?
What am I going to do first?
When am I going to do it?

Sometimes it can be scary or make us feel nervous when we think about letting people in our lives in a different way. We may have lots of thoughts or fears running through our minds when we think about this concept. Our fears, thoughts, and worries are always okay. We should give them space, and be real about them—but we should also know that our fears don't ever have to stop us from accomplishing great things and great relationships.

Brave Act

Get out the fears and worries and concerns. Write them all out, all over this page—then let them go. Don't let them control you, or stop you from making the relationships that could have the power to transform your life. Get those thoughts out, then keep moving.

Draw a picture of you with someone who
has made a difference in your life

Difference-maker

We all have biological parents. But who we call family doesn't have to be limited to feeling united and bonded with only with those who share our genetic makeup. There's a whole movement taking place on social media called #FamilyYouChoose.

No matter where you've come from, or what the status is with your bio fam, it's time to get connected.

Draw a picture with you in the center, then draw or write the names and descriptions of those you are connected to in the same way you could be connected to family. These can be friends, neighbors, distant relatives, cousins, friends from church, anyone—the sky is the limit! (Draw as many circles and lines as you'd like!)

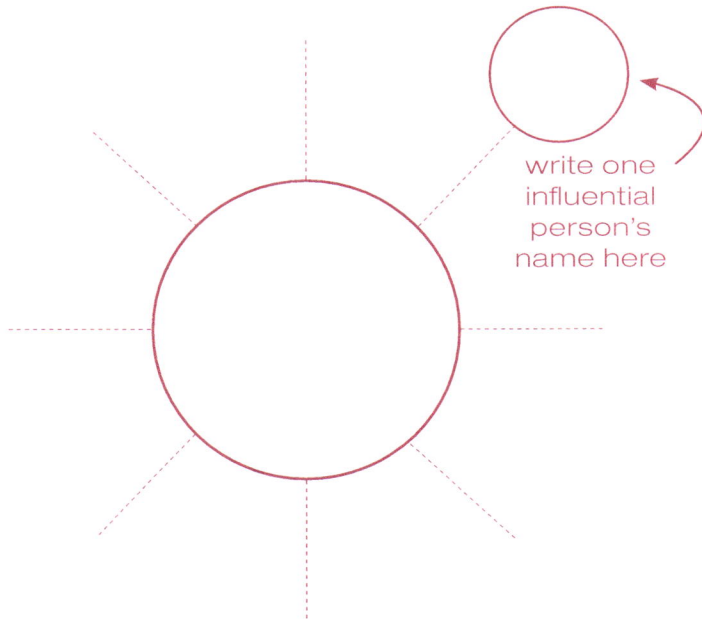

Brave Act

write one influential person's name here

There are places we can go, or things we can be a part of that put us in groups of people who can be a great substitute family. <u>A few examples are:</u> churches, clubs or groups, sport teams, etc.

Brave thought

Brave Act

Brainstorm something in your community that you can attend to be a part of something bigger. Write what this is, what would you need to do first, and a list of why this would be a good idea.

[Chapter 8]
Who Can We Look Up To?

Brave thought

>> THERE ARE PEOPLE OUT THERE WHO UNDER-STAND WHO WE ARE, WHERE WE COME FROM, AND WHY WE HURT. **There are people who have come up from ugly situations to become something great. Let's see into their lives, what makes them different, what makes us the same, and what makes them who they are.**

In this chapter, we want you to find a computer and look up the stories of some amazing women who have risen above ugly situations to become great, and healed people.

Agana *(street artist out of Oakland)* http://www.djagana.com
Nadia Bolz-Webber http://www.nadiabolzweber.com
Kat Von D http://www.thefamouspeople.com/profiles/kat-von-d-5554.php
Harmony Dust http://iamatreasure.com/about-harmony/
Here is a woman—**Nicole Lim**—who loves to tell the stories of incredible women in Africa. Check them out: http://www.freelyinhope.org

---

Find some more. This was just to get you started.

Not only that, but there are going to be some strong amazing women who are right around you. Take the time and initiative to interview them. Following is a list of sample questions to get your reporter career going.

Interview questions:

- What's your name?
- What do you do?
- What is your favorite thing to do for fun?
- What was your life like when you were a teen or preteen?
- What made a difference for you (the shift from victim to victor)?
- Who stood in the gap for you, or mentored you?
- What did you do to get through the really hard days?
- What would you say to a younger girl who is really struggling right now?

Ideas for people you could interview:

Brainstorm a bunch of women you look up to. Everyone's story
is not the same, so give folks a chance to tell you about themselves and
give you the keys to their success. You'll be amazed as you learn!

Interview

[Life Skills]
Practical Acts

This is here because I didn't realize how few practical life skills I had until
I was an adult. So many of the normal things that people knew how to do—I didn't!
So, some of this may reveal a little too much about my own background...
but some of it might actually be helpful! As a reminder, bravery is not just one
thing in our life, it is the everyday and ordinary of our lives.
So, find here some ideas to help you be brave in real life.

Thoughts? Notes?

Life Skill #1: How to cook eggs

**There are so many ways to cook eggs, which is great because
they are inexpensive and a good source of protein. Here are a few different ways.
Try them all, and see which one is your favorite.**

HARD-BOILED

INSTRUCTIONS:

1] Place eggs in saucepan large enough to hold them in single layer. Add cold water to cover eggs by 1 inch. Heat over high heat just to boiling.

2] Remove from burner. Cover pan. Let eggs stand in hot water about 12 minutes for large eggs (9 minutes for medium eggs; 15 minutes for extra large)

3] Drain immediately and serve warm. Or, cool completely under cold running water or in bowl of ice water, then eat or refrigerate.

SCRAMBLED

WHAT YOU NEED:
4 eggs
1/4 cup milk
Salt and pepper
2 tsp. butter

INSTRUCTIONS:

1] Beat eggs, milk, salt and pepper in bowl until blended.

2] Heat butter in large nonstick skillet over medium heat until hot. Pour in egg mixture.

3] As eggs begin to set, gently putll the eggs across the pan with a spatula, forming large soft curds. Continue cooking—pulling, lifting and folding eggs—until thickened and no visible liquid egg remains. Do not stir constantly. Remove from heat. Serve immediately.

FRIED

WHAT YOU NEED:
2-4 eggs
Butter
Salt and pepper

INSTRUCTIONS:
1] For over-easy or over-hard eggs: heat 2 tsp. butter in nonstick skillet over medium-high heat until hot.
2] Break eggs and slip into pan, 1 at a time. Immediately reduce heat to low.
3] Cook slowly until whites are completely set and yolks begin to thicken but are not hard. Slide spatula under each egg and carefully flip it over in pan. Cook second side to desired doneness. Sprinkle with salt and pepper. Serve immediately.

POACHED

INSTRUCTIONS:
1] Heat 2 to 3 inches of water and a dash of white vinegar in a large saucepan or deep skillet to boiling. Adjust heat to keep liquid simmering gently.
2] Break eggs, 1 at a time, into custard cup or saucer. Holding dish close to surface, slip egg into water.
3] Cook eggs until whites are completely set and yolks begin to thicken but are not hard, 3 to 5 minutes. Do not stir. Lift eggs from water with slotted spoon. Drain in spoon or on paper towels. Trim any rough edges, if desired. Sprinkle with salt and pepper. Serve immediately.

OMELET

WHAT YOU NEED:
2 eggs
2 tbsp. water
1/8 tsp. salt and dash pepper
1 tsp. butter
1/3 to 1/2 cup filling, such as shredded cheese, finely chopped ham, baby spinach

INSTRUCTIONS:
1] Beat eggs, water, salt and pepper in small bowl until blended.
2] Heat butter in 7 to 10-inch nonstick omelet pan or skillet over medium-high heat until hot. Tilt pan to coat bottom. Pour in egg mixture. Mixture should set immediately at edges.
3] Gently push cooked portions from edges toward the center with spatula so that uncooked eggs can reach the hot pan surface. Continue cooking, tilting pan and gently moving cooked portions as needed.
4] When top surface of eggs is thickened and no visible liquid egg remains, place filling on one side of the omelet. Fold omelet in half with spatula. With a quick flip of the wrist, turn pan and flip or slide omelet onto plate. Serve immediately.

FRITTATA

WHAT YOU NEED:
4 eggs
1/4 cup liquid, such as milk, tomato juice, broth
1/4 tsp. dried thyme leaves or herb of your choice
Salt and pepper
1 cup filling such as broccoli, red onion and cheese
2 tsp. butter or vegetable oil

INSTRUCTIONS:

1] Beat eggs, liquid, herb and salt and pepper in medium bowl until blended. Add filling; mix well. Heat butter in large nonstick skillet over medium heat until hot. Pour in egg mixture.

2] Heat butter in 6 to 8-inch nonstick omelet pan or skillet over medium heat until melted. Pour in egg mixture; cook over low to medium heat until eggs are almost set.

3] Remove from heat. Cover and let stand until eggs are completely set and no visible liquid egg remains, 5 to 10 minutes.

FRENCH TOAST

WHAT YOU NEED:
8 eggs
1/3 cup milk
1/4 tsp. ground nutmeg, optional
8 day-old bread slices

INSTRUCTIONS:

1] Beat eggs, milk and nutmeg in shallow dish until blended. Soak 1 bread slice at a time in egg mixture, turning once, letting stand about 1 minute per side.

2] Heat lightly-greased large nonstick skillet over high heat until hot. Remove from heat.

3] Place as many bread slices in hot pan as will fit in single layer. Immediately reduce heat to medium. Cook until golden brown and no visible liquid egg remains, 2 to 3 minutes per side. Repeat to cook remaining bread. Serve immediately.

*These instructions were taken from http://www.incredibleegg.org/cooking-school/egg-cookery/

Life Skill #2: How to do laundry

STEP 1: Sort Your clothes

Separate your laundry into piles of whites, light colors, dark colors and linens (like sheets, towels and blankets). Don't mix light and dark colors together. Even if the clothes have been washed many times, bright colors will fade and lighter colors will get dingy or gray.

STEP 2: Check the labels

When learning how to do laundry, look at the labels of each of the clothes. If a label says: "hand wash only," "dry clean only," or "wash separately," put it aside in a "special care" pile.

WASHING SYMBOLS

GENERAL
- Machine wash
- Hand wash
- Do not wash
- Dry clean only
- Do not dry clean

TEMPERATURE
- Wash cold
- Wash warm
- Wash hot

MACHINE CYCLES
- Normal cycle
- Permanent press cycle
- Delicate / gentle cycle

BLEACHING SYMBOLS
- Bleaching allowed
- Do not bleach
- Use non-chlorine bleach

DRYING SYMBOLS

GENERAL
- Tumble drying allowed
- Do not tumble dry
- Hang to dry
- Dry flat
- Do not wring

TEMPERATURE
- Any heat
- Low heat
- Medium heat
- High heat
- No heat / air

TUMBLE DRY CYCLES
- Normal cycle
- Permanent press cycle
- Delicate / gentle cycle

IRONING SYMBOLS
- Iron low
- Iron medium
- Iron high
- Do not iron
- No steam added to iron

https://tide.com/en-us

BRAVE 2018

STEP 3: Check the clothes

One of the most important steps when learning how to do the laundry is to empty all pockets. Remove all accessories like belts or pins. Check everything for stains. Stains like grass, blood, dirt, sweat and food should be pre-treated with a stain remover. Follow instructions on your stain removal product. It usually needs to be sprayed, rubbed or soaked, depending on the type of stain and product you're using.

STEP 4: Set the washer

On the washing machine you will find dials or buttons for choosing the type of water and cycle appropriate for your laundry load.
—**Warm water** is used for most loads. Use it for light- and bright-colored clothes, cottons and linens, jeans, and most regular-wash clothes.
—**Cold water** is best for light colors and delicate things—swimwear, bras, and workout clothes. When you're not sure how to do the laundry, use the cold water, delicate setting. If you don't have too many delicates, hand-wash instead.
—**Hot water** is best for removing stains and germs from clothes and can be used for white clothes and light-colored linens. However, hot water isn't very gentle to fabrics or color. It can make them shrink, fade or wear out.

STEP 5: Start the washer

Turn on the machine and let it start filling with water before you add the clothes. (If you have a front-loading machine, this isn't possible, so turn it on only after you load the clothes.) Measure and add the detergent, following the instructions on the container. If you are washing bright colors, you can add color-safe bleach or detergent with bleach alternatives. If you are washing whites in hot water and all of the washing instructions on your clothing tags agree, add a small amount of bleach to the water before adding your clothes. Make sure to wipe up any spills with a wet sponge or paper towel, and be sure not to spill any on your clothing as it will ruin it.

STEP 6: Load the washer

Place one pile of clothes into the washer. Leave enough room for the clothes to move around in the washer. Do not overfill or your clothes won't get clean. Close the lid and wait for it to finish. Start the washer if you haven't already and wait for it to finish.

STEP 7: Dry the clothes

Remove clothes from the washer as soon as the full cycle is done. The washer will go through a few cycles of starts and stops, so check the dial or display to tell you when it's finished. Some washers will beep when they're done. If clothes are left in the washer for more than a few hours, they could become stinky and need to be rewashed before drying. Empty the lint filter on the dryer before each load. If you don't, it could become a fire hazard.

One important thing to remember when learning how to do the laundry is to check the washing instructions on each piece of clothing. They will say something like: "hang dry," "lay flat to dry," "tumble dry low heat," "tumble dry remove promptly." Follow all instructions and load dryer-safe clothes into the dryer, being sure not to overstuff the dryer or your clothes won't dry properly. If clothes are not dryer safe, follow instructions on the tags for best results.

Turn on the dryer and follow the instructions on the clothing tags and the dryer to choose the best setting for your load. As soon as the dryer is done, empty it and fold clothes to avoid wrinkles.

*These instructions were taken from http://www.beinggirl.com/article/how-to-do-the-laundry/

Life Skill #3: How to apply for a job

Its time to find a job! You are old enough, you are ready, time to get prepared. Here's how to find a job in 8 easy steps.

STEP 1: Get all your info together.

To find a job you will need some personal information. You will need things like your social security card. Knowing the number without the actual card won't be enough, so make sure to have a copy of this on hand. You will also need a passport, driver's license, or some form of ID with your picture on it. Also depending on your age and the state you live in, you might need a work permit.

STEP 2: Put a resume together!

Most teens looking for a job don't make one, and you can get by without it, but by having a resume it will put you ahead of the game of others that are trying to get the same job you are. This website will help you with the info you need to build a resume; https://www.livecareer.com/quintessential/teen-resume-writing-worksheet

STEP 3: What are you going to wear?

You don't need to be in a fancy dress, but you do need to look professional. There are lots of options at thrift stores for basic items that are cheap, and will look like you are ready to land this job, and do your best.

STEP 4: Short term or long term?

Do you want a job for the short term, something that isn't in your career field, or the area of work you are dreaming of—just something to get you through now, like a fast food job, or something in the mall? These are good options for teens, but you could find something in your field that you want to do forever. Remember to explore all your options.

STEP 5: What are you going to say?

Look online for common interview questions, and be prepared with your answers. You don't want to sound reversed or fake, but it can be hard to think quickly and articulately on your feet. Plan ahead for how you will answer these, and how you will describe yourself. If you aren't used to saying words like sir or ma'am, please and thank you, practice saying them out loud so you are used to hearing yourself say them before the interview. Always use the best manners possible.

STEP 6: You probably aren't the only one applying for this job.

Expect there to be competition, and even a few jobs you apply for that you wont get. That's okay and just a part of the process. Don't get discouraged and give up, even if it takes longer than you'd like it to.

STEP 7: Call them before they call you.

Your level of professionalism will show in your followthrough, even before you have the job. Call and ask to speak to the manager. Ask them if they have had a chance to review your application, and if you haven't yet, ask if there is a time to schedule and interview. Be assertive and confident, not bossy or rude. Also, no matter the outcome, it would be a great idea to send out thank you notes either hand written and delivered to the manager, or via email if you have it. Thanking the person for their time and consideration for your application. This kind of gesture might help you get a job their in the future, even if the current one you are trying to get doesn't work out.

STEP 8: Make a plan to succeed!

You get the job! Now make a plan on how you will do your best. So many people lose their jobs because they are late. One saying that can be really helpful is, "5 min early is on time, on time is late, and late is never acceptable."

Plan on how you will dress, how you will treat others around you, how you will do the things you are asked to do—even if you don't want to. Do every thing on purpose.

You can do this! Good luck!

Life Skill #4:
How to cook in the microwave

**You can use the microwave for more than just heating things up.
What can you cook with a microwave?**

CAKE IN A CUP

WHAT YOU NEED:
1/4 cup all-purpose flour
2 tbsp. unsweetened cocoa powder
1/4 tsp. baking powder
2 tbsp. granulated sugar (you can add 1 tbsp. more if you like it sweeter)
1/4 tsp. salt
1/4 cup + 1 tbsp. milk
2 tbsp. vegetable oil
1 tbsp. hazelnut chocolate spread

INSTRUCTIONS:
1] In a medium bowl, whisk together dry ingredients.
2] Whisk in the milk and vegetable oil until all ingredients are combined and batter has no clumps. Pour batter into a microwave-safe mug. Mine was a 14-ounce mug. You want enough head space for the cake to rise without pouring over.
3] Add 1 tbsp. of hazelnut chocolate spread in the middle of the batter. Just drop it in the middle, no need to push it down and sink it in the batter.
4] Place a paper towel into the microwave and set the mug on top (this is to catch any batter if your mug cake overflows).
5] Microwave mug cake for 70 seconds on high.
6] Carefully remove from microwave and enjoy!

STEAMING VEGGIES

INSTRUCTIONS:
(This works well with: carrots, broccoli, asparagus, green beans, peas and bell peppers)

1] Wash and dry your vegetable and cut it into equal size pieces.
2] Place them in one layer in a microwave safe glass bowl or a dish with sides.
3] Add just enough water to the bowl that it comes 1/8 up the side of the vegetable piece.
4] Cover the bowl with plastic wrap or a microwave safe cover, and microwave for 2 minutes. Test the vegetable for softness, and rotate or flip it if necessary. Cook again for four minutes.
5] Continue alternating sides and cooking for one minute per side until the vegetable can easily be pierced with a fork. Once your veggies are moist and tender, they are all ready to serve!

COOKING CHICKEN BREAST

WHAT YOU NEED:
1½ pounds boneless, skinless chicken breast halves

INSTRUCTIONS:
1] Arrange chicken, thickest parts to outside edges in glass pie plate, 10 x 1½ or 9 x 1¼ inches (sides of chicken will touch).
2] Cover dish with plastic wrap, folding back one corner or edge 1/4 inch to vent steam. Microwave on Medium (50%) 14 to 16 minutes or until juice of chicken is no longer pink when center of thickest pieces are cut and temperature reaches 170°. Let stand 5 minutes.
3] Cool slightly; cut into desired size of pieces.

MAKING A BAKED POTATO

WHAT YOU NEED:
1 to 4 russet potatoes
Olive oil
Salt
Pepper

EQUIPMENT:
Fork
Microwave-safe plate or baking dish
Oven mitts

INSTRUCTIONS:
1] Scrub the potatoes clean: Scrub the potatoes thoroughly under running water and pat them dry. You don't have to remove the eyes, but trim away any blemishes with a paring knife. Pat dry.
2] Pierce with a fork: Prick the potatoes four or five times on each side with a fork. This allows steam to escape from the baking potato.
3] Rub with olive oil, salt, and pepper: Rub the potatoes all over with a little olive oil. Generously sprinkle the potatoes with salt and pepper.
4] Microwave for 5 minutes: Place the potatoes in a microwave-safe dish and microwave at full power for 5 minutes.
5] Flip the potatoes: Use a fork or tongs to flip the potatoes—they will be hot. If you remove the dish from the microwave, use oven mitts, as the dish will be hot.
6] Continue microwaving the potatoes: If cooking one potato, microwave for an additional 3 minutes. If cooking two or more potatoes, microwave an additional 5 minutes.
7] Check the potatoes: When done, the potatoes should be easily pierced with a fork or paring knife all the way to the center. Continue to microwave in 1-minute bursts as needed until the

potatoes are cooked through. Use oven mitts to remove the dish from the microwave.

8] OPTIONAL—Crisp the potatoes in the oven: If you'd like crispier skin, heat the oven to 425°F while the potatoes are microwaving, then transfer them to the oven to roast. Check every few minutes and remove once the skin is dry and crisped.

9] Serve the potatoes: Let the potatoes cool briefly, then serve. Potatoes can also be cooled completely and refrigerated for up to 4 days; reheat in the microwave or in the oven.

Life Skill #5:
How to manage money

Here is a life hack you've got to read:

http://lifehacker.com/how-to-manage-your-money-for-those-who-never-learned-g-1703892260

Write about what you learned

Life Skill #6:
How to get organized

1] Organize for 15 minutes each day. This could mean anything from sorting mail to throwing out mystery foods in the refrigerator. Just 15 minutes a day can make a huge difference over time.

2] **3 most important tasks:** Writing down and making mental note of my top 3 tasks to get done for the day. Everything else seems to fall into place if I do that.

3] An easy and workable task list, or to do list. Instead of staying up at night with things rotating around your brain—write them down. The list will not only help you sleep but keep you on track with your life.

4] Do one thing at a time. And try to 'do it now'. Whatever is next on the list—just do it. Don't think about it too much.

5] Make use of the word no. Really. You don't have to do everything.

6] Get a calendar and **write in your priorities first.** The things that are most important for your life goals.

Life Skill #7: Healthy Habits

FOODS TO EAT

Some foods can help protect your health. Try to focus more on these foods.

Fruits and vegetables are packed with vitamins and minerals. They also have fiber, which helps you feel full and is great for you. Try to fill half your plate with a variety of different fruits and veggies. And instead of drinking juice, try to munch on whole fruits, whether frozen, canned, or dried.

Whole grains have lots of health benefits, including possibly helping prevent heart disease. At least half your grains should be whole grains. This includes whole wheat, oatmeal, and brown rice. (It even includes popcorn—just watch out for added butter and salt.)

Fat-free and low-fat milk products are great. They are especially good for a girl during her childhood and teen years because she needs them to build strong bones. Look for fat-free or low-fat cheese, yogurt, and other dairy products. If you can't drink milk, try soy drinks fortified with calcium and vitamin D.

Protein helps your body heal, gives you energy, and more. Choose a mix of different protein foods. Good options include fish and other seafood, poultry (without the skin), lean meats, beans and peas, eggs, soy products, and unsalted nuts and seeds. Try to pick fish and shellfish in place of some meat and poultry.

You can get great tips on ways to fill your plate with healthy foods.

WHO DECIDES WHAT'S HEALTHY?

You may wonder who figures out what you should eat. (Well, other than maybe your parents!) Every few years the government brings together experts to look at recent nutrition research. Then they create the Dietary Guidelines for Americans to make suggestions for the health of people throughout the country.

Foods to limit Some foods are not good for your health if you eat too much of them. Try to have less of these.

Solid fats, which are fats that are solid at room temperature. Solid fats usually are high in saturated fat and trans fat, and eating too much of them can cause problems like heart disease. Oils that have unsaturated fat are a much healthier choice. Learn more about the different kinds of fats and the recommended amounts to eat.

Sodium is found in table salt and lots of prepared foods. Eating too much sodium can cause health problems such as high blood pressure. Get the lowdown on sodium.

Added sugars mean you're getting extra calories without any extra nutrients. Added sugars are often hiding out in your soda, cookies, candy, and sugary cereals. Read more about sugars and other carbohydrates.

Refined grains are grains that have had some of the nutrients removed. Choose whole grains because they have all the nutrients.

Cholesterol can increase your risk of heart disease. Check the Nutrition Facts label on foods you eat to see how much cholesterol they have. Try to eat as little cholesterol as possible. Cholesterol usually comes from foods like ice cream, steak, and other animal products.

HOW MUCH FOOD DO YOU NEED TO EAT?

Eating a healthy amount of food helps your body do all the important jobs it needs to do. Eating a lot more than you need or not eating enough can prevent your body from working well.

Eating too much or too little also can stop you from being at a healthy weight. How much you need to eat depends on things like your age, sex, and how active you are. Learn more about being at a healthy weight and about why calories count.

Your body also needs a healthy mix of foods. For example, your body can't work well if you eat piles of protein and little else. The MyPlate food guide can help you figure out how much of each type of food you need.

*This was taken from http://girlshealth.gov/nutrition/healthy_eating/index.html

HOW DO WE EAT A BALANCED DIET?

There are five food groups. And the easiest way to eat a well balanced diet is to make sure that you have the right portions of food groups every day (notice sugar is not a food group) ;-)

Grains. 6 servings a day. Try to eat whole grains instead of white, starchy stuff.
Fruits. 4 servings a day. Lots of different colors.
Vegetables. 3-4 servings a day. Lots of different colors.
Dairy. 3 servings a day.
Meat. No more than 3-6 ounces per day (that's like the size of your palm).

HOW MUCH EXERCISE DO WE NEED, AND WHY DO WE NEED IT?

Exercise not only is good for your physical health—it's also good for your brain and your emotional health. It's the way your body de-stressed itself. In other words, if you find yourself struggling with stress (tired/depressed/anxious) it could help you to keep physically active.

The best way to do this is to do something fairly basic every day (walk/run/gym). Even 30 minutes a day will really make a big difference.

WHY SHOULD WE AVOID DRUGS AND DRINKING?

This is the easiest and most common stress reliever for a lot of people. The trouble is that it really isn't. It makes you feel like stress is leaving but it also adds stress to your life. It is really just a 'delay' and because it 'delays' the inevitable realities of your life it actually adds stress. This is the last thing you need to make healthy choices. It can be a tempting option—but it never, ever works. Look at the evidence.

Life Skill #8:
Dealing with drama and conflict

There is always going to be conflict. When it happens, what do we do about it? We all experience disagreements and drama. When this happens with you and a peer, there are a few steps that we can take to resolve it for real, not just to sweep it under the rug, or ignore the issue. These aren't always easy, but if we do them honestly, then it can be amazing how things are truly resolved.

STEP 1: Agree to work together. Set some ground rules, like no name-calling or put-downs, no making fun of each other, or talking back about each other, or others that may not be present.

STEP 2: Hear everyone's side. Start with one person going first, maybe even rock-paper- scissors to see who gets to go first so there is no disagreements about that. Then whomever is speaking gets to say all of their side of the story without being interrupted. even if you think they are wrong, or lying, or confused, or anything like that. The point of this is that everyone gets to be heard. One person goes, and then as the person who is listening, before they say their side they have to say what they heard the first person say without correcting or arguing. Repeating what you heard makes the person sharing feel heard, and helps reduce anger.

Each person gets a chance to do that process.

STEP 3: After each person has shared their side, the other has repeated what they heard, then you get a chance to find the parts that everyone agrees on. What is the mutual problem, and what needs to be done to fix it on both sides. What are interests that everyone has that they want to strive toward?

STEP 4: Use "I" statements. I feel, I think, etc. that way people don't feel blamed—we are sharing our feelings instead of pointing fingers.

STEP 5: Brainstorm ways that things can be resolved. Do people need to apologize, or admit fault to another party? Sometimes we can agree to disagree, but there might be solutions that we can all agree on.

STEP 6: Make an agreement. Really decide how things are going to be resolved. It may even be helpful to write them down so everyone knows what is up, and that it can end with people feeling genuinely heard, and with a plan on how to move forward.

When we do this we may not get our way all of the time, but resolving the conflict and reducing the drama is way better than getting your way. It will strengthen relationships, and help us grow together.

Read more at: http://www.helpguide.org/articles/relationships/conflictresolution-skills.htm

HOW TO PROTEST, WHEN THINGS ARE WRONG

Sometimes things are so wrong that you need to do something about it. Seriously. So here is a quick list to help you with that course of action should it be necessary.

1] Stay calm and be very clear about the details of the situation.
2] Speak with a decision maker. (this might take some research on your part but it's useless to protest with someone who has no power to change the situation—it will just frustrate you).
3] Write down your goal/necessary changes for you to be safe.
4] Come to the meeting/phone call/letter prepared—write down what you want to say so you don't get side-tracked by emotions.

5] Explain your situation clearly, and include your goals.

6] Give the person you are speaking to a time-line to get back to you. ('When can I expect to hear back from you?)

7] If they don't get back to you—find someone over them and start the process again. You'd be surprised at how often this happens in loads of different areas.

8] If there still is no response you may need to get some others who have similar problems together and consider hiring a lawyer/or going to the media/ or a public demonstration.

Life Skill #9:
Manners and kindness

Here are some basic manners—not all are needed in every situation. But this is a good list to start with, especially during school or when interacting at a job, or with adults.

- Say 'please' and 'thank you' whenever you have a chance. This shows people that we care about them, and have respect for them.
- Apologize when we have done something wrong, or have done something that maybe we don't think is wrong but has hurt someone else.
- Keep your hands to yourself. We don't need to touch or push in ways that cause pain or make people feel uncomfortable. This goes for people, and people's things. Touch is something that is used to ex press kindness when the person doing the touching has permission. Things like side hugs, and high fives are a great way to do this.
- When someone else is talking, try not to interrupt.
- If you need to get someones attention, or have bumped into them— say 'excuse me'.
- If we want something, or want to do something—we should ask for permission.
- If someone gives us something or does something nice for us, we should send them a thank you note.
- When we are having a conversation or meeting someone for the first time, look them in the eye. Shake hands with a firm grip.
- We may have negative options of people or situations—it's best to keep these to ourselves. We may feel tempted to make fun of others, but this can be hurtful and lead to damaged relationships.
- Try not to act like we are bored, even if we are super bored.
- If we cough or sneeze, we should cover our face with the inside of our elbows instead of our hands. This helps us to not spread germs.
- Try not to talk with food in our mouths.

Life Skill #10:
Living a spiritual life

The writer of this journal is a follower of Jesus, so my view on what living a spiritual life looks like is through the lens of Jesus.

How do we live a spiritual life with intentionality?

Pray—prayer is just talking to God. We don't have to use fancy words, or even have a lot to say at once. We can just talk to God like we talk to our friends. God is okay with our feelings, with our fear, or with our questions. He is bigger than any of those things and just wants to hear us.

Read scripture—Reading the Bible teaches us about who we are as we learn about the one that created us. It shows us God's love, and how much he wants to be in a relationship with us. That is where we find the truth, and have our questions answered. I suggest starting with the words of Jesus—those are the Gospels. They are the books of the Bible called Matthew, Mark, Luke and John.

Meditate—This means spending time in quiet reflection. Maybe you do this while reading or drawing. Maybe just sitting quietly. This practice helps us find peace and a sense of calmness.

Unite with other believers (church, Bible studies, other groups)—Be a part of something bigger. We don't have to go to church to be Christians, but it really helps. We go to church to be in community together. We go to lean on each other for our burdens or tough times. We go so others can be that for us, and we can be that for them too.

Have faith in what you cannot see—There will be a lot of things that happen in this life that we don't like or understand. But we believe that God is in charge of it all. We believe that He has our back through it all, and that He sent his son Jesus to die for us to have a chance to live freely, and we believe that God sent the Holy Spirit to walk with us every day to be our comforter and our guide. You aren't alone!

Check out infinitumlife.com for helpful tips on how to get started.

Hope is being able
to see that there is
light despite all
of the darkness.

— Desmond Tutu

Final Thoughts

This is the end of Journal #1, but hopefully it's just the start of your journey to be BRAVE. Most likely, you got this journal because you attended an event called BRAVE at a church near you. That church exists for you. We want to make sure that you know you are welcome, needed, wanted and loved there. All of us are looking for a place to belong. You can belong there. Be brave and join in as we discover that we get braver when we stand together.

A couple of final

Brave thoughts

1] Keep journaling. There will be more journals like this one. But get your own. Start writing everyday and keep practicing the things you've learned. Practice really does make perfect.

2] Get in a good group. Hang with some sisters who are also trying to be brave. We need each other. That's the first brave admission. No one can be truly brave alone.

3] Pray. If you haven't discovered that God loves you and Jesus is your friend now is a great time. You are not alone. He knows you. You can't do this alone and you don't have to. Why not take some time even right now to commit your life to follow Jesus. Ask Him to give you the courage and strength you need to live bravely. Ask him to give you a fresh start. Then get ready for some adventure. How 'bout a prayer like this: "Jesus, thanks for coming to earth to tell me that you haven't forgotten me. That you will never leave me. That you know what it is to suffer. That you want me to be free. Please forgive me. Please give me a new start. Fill me with your strength and courage and power to be brave. To live a life of freedom and hope. I choose to follow you today. Thanks for inviting me into a brave life. Amen."

4] Keep coming back. This process of Bravery in real life takes a lot of effort. Don't be discouraged from trying again and again. The bravest people I know are the ones who get back up after they fall down and try again. Keep trying again. Go to another Brave event. Find a support group. Start the journal over. Pray. Repeat. You are already doing amazing to get this far. We are so proud of you.

Psalm 139:13-16, The Message

"Oh yes, you shaped me first inside, then out;
you formed me in my mother's womb.
I thank you, High God—you're breathtaking!
Body and soul, I am marvelously made!
I worship in adoration—what a creation!
You know me inside and out,
you know every bone in my body;
You know exactly how I was made, bit by bit,
how I was sculpted from nothing into something.
Like an open book, you watched me grow
from conception to birth;
all the stages of my life were spread out
before you,
The days of my life all prepared
before I'd even lived one day."